All Me

Stefanie Amey

BookLeaf Publishing

India | USA | UK

All Me © 2022

Stefanie Amey

Presentation by *BookLeaf Publishing*

Web: www.bookleafpub.com

E-mail: info@bookleafpub.com

ISBN : 9789358365535

First edition 2022

Acknowledgements

One of the greatest gifts you can give
someone is inspiration.
Thank you to all who have given me mine.

Mom, my biggest supporter and number one
fan, your love is truly unconditional. Thank
you for your incredible heart and giving me
the courage to follow my dreams.

Dad, thank you for all of your stories and for
always knowing how to make me laugh.

My family without whom, I would not be
me. Thank you for everything.

The artists of the world, the writers, the
actors, the musicians for marking the road
ahead and creating a world filled with
beauty, thank you.

Special thanks to BookLeaf Publishing.

Preface

What started as a way to challenge myself, has now become a personal passion project that I am immensely proud of.

The title "All Me" doesn't suggest that these poems are all about myself specifically, but rather the act of writing and putting together this book is the first accomplishment in my life that has been completed one hundred percent on my own without the input, thoughts or opinions of other people. "All Me" is a work all my own. Writing these poems has been an exploration in finding myself and allowing myself the possibility and the space to fail while also providing me with room to grow. It has been a liberating experience, giving me the realization that you don't have to be perfect in order to feel and be seen.

The words written within this book are inspired by simple everyday moments that although are personal to me, I feel have a universal quality. For it is the simple moments, the small and mundane, that sometimes have the greatest and most profound effects on our lives. I hope you, dear reader, feel as great an impact reading these poems as I did writing them.

Cracks and crevices,
muddied, muddled perception,
hiding the world from my strangled
perfection.
Pure, perfect loveliness
no room for error
the mirrored flaw screams in terror
Conceal! Conceal! Conceal!
Never reveal!

- Mask

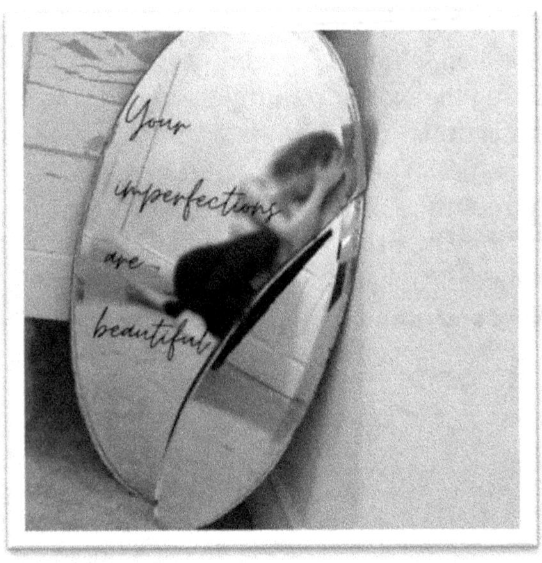
Your
imperfections
are
beautiful

I don't like all the people,
I like to be alone;
you see, I've always been so happy
by myself at home.

When the people come to visit,
they really stress me out;
they're messy, loud and busy
and really wear me out.

Their hugs are overbearing,
their children are obscene;
they barge their way into my space,
they really are quite mean.

They're noisy, obnoxious tyrants,
they destroy my tidy home;
when the people come a calling,
oh how I yearn to be left alone.

I like my quiet home,
I do things just for me;
I like to sit with cozy blankets
and sip a quiet tea,

I love all of the silence,
it's really quite serene;
I feel at my best
sitting here just with me.

When the people finally leave,
I jump and shout out "yes!"
The quiet has returned
and I can finally have a rest.

The people are all gone,
the silence has returned,
but as I sit here by myself,
for something, I still yearn.

What is this feeling?
What could this be?
I wanted them to leave,
but as I look around my home,
it now feels rather empty.

I miss the peoples' laughter,
their playing and happy shrieks;
I miss the crazy children,
dear Lord! What is happening to me?

I miss the fun and games we play
and when I don't feel so alone,
but most of all I miss the people,
for the people are my home.

- The People

In the darkness now,
we come to see the lighthouse
momentarily.

Perpetually
dark receding waves upon
rocks jagged blackness.

Lighthouse o lighthouse,
no longer, fading, lighting
momentarily.

- Lighthouse

Darkness is only
temporary

Delicate beauties,
withering moments,
a touch, a whisper, a word

brushed across lips soft,
feathery stillness;
an eyelash that falls
from the cheek.

Fragrant lavender
in cooling tea.
Quiet tapping fingers.
A long embrace.

- The Peaceful Goodbye

Oh the Rose Campion
covered in fuzz,
with petals of fuchsia
that everyone loves.
But wait, it's magenta!
Or maybe just pink?
They're all the same colour
I'd like to think.

What is a Rose Campion?
It's certainly no rose;
Mullein-pink,
Bloody William,
Or Dusty Miller
as it's commonly known.

Oh dear I forgot
Lambs Ear it is not.
I tell you it's true!
Lambs Ear has no colourful hue.
Like the pretty Rose Campion
With its pink petal flowers;
when in bloom, the bees do devour.

As I told you before,
I will tell you again;
so before you forget,
quick, grab a pen!
With its grey felted leaves
though it does appear,

Rose campion is not the same
as Lambs Ear!

- Rose Campion

- The Panic

A thought, a feeling,
a stolen sigh.
The beat between
two lungs;
breath stealing wind,
wind stealing breath,
stealing space, stealing life,
Stealing;
In
Out
In
Out
Stealing;
In
Out
In
Out
Breathing;
In
Out
In
Out
Gasping!
In, out
In, out!
BURNING!
In! Out!
In! Out!
In! Out!

CHOKING!!!
IN! OUT!
iNOuT!
in! oUT!
In OUt!
iN! OUT!
IN ouT!
IN! OUT!
IN OUT!
Slowing!
In! Out!
In! Out!
Slowing;
In
Out
In
Out
Slowing;
In
Out
In
Out
Steady;
In
Out

In

Out

Quiet;

In

Out

In

Out

Tired;

In

Out

In

Out

Ending;

In

Out

In

Out

Peaceful;

in

out

in

out,

in

out

in

out…

finally.

Breathe

What's wrong with you?
Why is a little child
not playful and wild?
Why are you so quiet and out of view?
Are you okay? Do you want to play? Go, go,
here's a gentle nudge,
the other kids are lots of fun.
What's wrong with you?

What's wrong with you?
Why can't you be more?
Be the right amount of cute,
of sweet, of lovable?
A perfect recipe.
Why can't you be more like her,
that other little girl?
Why don't you show off your curls?
And be fun and outgoing too?
Seriously, what's wrong with you?

What's wrong with you?
Why don't you want to go to school?
Why aren't you making friends?
I'm sorry you're crying, I am trying;
to understand and care
but life's not fair
so pick yourself up and get out there.
You know I love you,
What's wrong with you?

What's wrong with you?
Why are you here?
Do you just need an ear
to listen and clear?
the cobwebs that linger,
the memories that hinder
an ideal future?
Tell me, what's wrong with you?

What's wrong with you?
Don't you have a partner? Or a suitor?
A young lady like you
should certainly have a few.
Why don't you smile?
You're only young for a while;
like clay on a wheel,
useful until the water runs out;
a clock ticking down to the final drought.
Better get a man
while you still can.
Why don't you show some skin?
That'll help you win
the relationship lottery
and mould yourself into perfect pottery;
don't you want a perfect family?
What's wrong with you?

What's wrong with you?!
Like a fool, I've listened to your
condescending and cruel
words magnified by your own hurt.

But don't you see?
Repeating "concerns"
make a girl start to question
what's wrong with me?
Just another sad story
with tragedies
that would have been easier
had you been a little more accepting.
A lesson learned of that I'm sure, a subtle
plea to stop questioning
and let a life just be.

- The Voices

I'm that girl
whose name you don't remember.
A random face taking up space
that you never see
or ever care to look for.
When you hear my voice, it is drowning in a
sea of thousands much louder,
you don't hear me at all.
My words don't hit you the way they
should, the way I want them to,
I want you to be hit with the force of my
feeling, to have the wind knocked from your
lungs.
As you lay gasping like a fish choking on
air, I want you to know the feeling
of not being seen,
of not being heard,
of being ignored;
while you writhe in pain,
maybe then
you will remember
my name

- *My Name*

Muses musing time,
here, timelines ever-changing
days, months, years, decades…

> Turning centuries
> longing to be held in a
> moment's embrace. Stay.

- Time

The man in the window
stares blankly into the street,
his tired grey eyes bleak.
A hunched silhouette,
a black and white photo,
his dreams are the colour of his hair;
smoke, wispy, disappearing,
swirling tendrils of silver blue;
his memory lingers on
like a phantom limb,
painful in its desire to be cradled.
Pins and pine needles stabbing,
aching for a life that used to be.
Burning embers stubbed into a lifeless ash
dusted white, chalky;
A home he can't regain,
staring through the window,
staring through the pain.

- *Window pain*

Mother is letting me go.
I can feel her pulling away from me.
My veins are drying, shrinking;
my skin has started to shrivel,
withered at the edges.
I remember the days of being
small and full of life,
how the sun's warmth was endless,
the rain soft and sweet.
The rain made mother happy;
the water sank into her
and she seemed to sing with bliss.
I felt her song nourish me as I waved to
her alongside my brothers and sisters,
her arms stretched
towards the heavens as she held us,
swaying and dancing with the wind.
The warm memories only make the brisk,
sharp bite of the cold all the more frigid.
My brothers and sisters; a rainbow
palette of gold laid to rest below me,
I remain, enduring.
I hear mother groan and creak under the
weight of the air as she tries to hold onto
me. Though she stands proud and sturdy,
she is freezing.
It is time to let go.
I feel the wind coming;
it lifts under me as I stretch my frail body
upwards to wave one last time to mother.

The final blow,
before the fall.

-The Fall

Holding on
is sometimes harder
than letting go

I wonder about the stars,
I wonder about God and the universe;
I wonder what we are to him,
I wonder if maybe the sun
isn't a sun at all
but a hole, a doorway into the light of
another world.
I think maybe the sun is God's eye and
that we are the world as he sees it;
a hologram, an upside-down image of his
own reality.
Perhaps our earth is the rich, beautiful
colour of the iris of God; a swirling orb of
blue and gold and green.
Perhaps we are the centre of his eye's
pupillated blackness,
our moon the lens
in which his light is reflected.
Perhaps God has many eyes.
Perhaps the entirety of space and time
as we know it, is the living, breathing body
of God and the planets, stars, and galaxies
are his cells, his blood, his pure essence;
what a wonderful notion,
for what could be more beautiful than
a god made of stars.

- A God Made of Stars

Sunday country
filled with lemony light;
that these shy poppies would choose to
bloom, their courage growing through the
night.
A father's song that plays paves the way
for memories of red wagons and
entwined hands;
how the daisies sway in that filtered
light, their golden faces laughing,
their petaled hair curling behind them as
stories told remember an old life in Sunday
country.

- *Sunday Country*

You look like me
and I talk like you;
you walk like her,
and I do too.

So does she, and we can all be
mistaken for one another
every once in a while
because we all pretty much have the
same style.

We have the same hair
but we like different things.
We never like to share;
I'm usually nice
but you keep stealing my underwear!

Do you girls remember those days
that now feel so far away?
How we couldn't stand each other
but together we'd always play—

Hide and seek
and horsing around
and when we got tired,
we'd lay on the ground.

Oh us girls,
always in cohorts;
running around in backwoods
and building secret forts.

Do you remember the good old days?
The really great times?
The "GIVE ME THAT BACK's!"
And the "NO! IT'S MINE's!"

The pinky promises
and little white lies,
the cross my heart
and hope to dies'

Remember our backyard?
And how we'd stare up at the stars?
When we were all together,
I felt the universe in my heart.

I miss all you girls, I really do
and sometimes I think,
you really miss me too.

We've all got our lives now,
living miles and miles apart
but I always think of you three,
you're always in my heart.

Someday we'll all hang out again
and we can pretend
to be little for awhile,
like how we used to giggle and smile.

Like how the spring returns
after a long winter,

we'll be home again someday
with each other.
My best friends,
my sisters.

- Home Again

Home is found
within each other

Stupid fat moon
in the sky,
I wonder why
people swoon over you.

You just hang there
in the air
with your stupid stare
that glares
over every one of us fools,
Stupid fat moon.

Stupid fat moon;
you're such a pain,
the way you wax and wane.
A fickle lover
the way you hover.

And do you think it's right
that your bright light
steals the night
and drowns out the stars?
Who do you think you are?
Stupid fat moon.

Stupid fat moon;
controlling and tidal,
you think you're entitled
to be so lazy and idle
why won't you move?

What are you trying to prove you huge
Stupid fat moon?

Stupid fat moon;
I don't understand
why the world thinks you so grand,
they all talk of "the man in the moon"

I really can't stand
all your adoring fans,
am I the only one who's immune?
You're just a big
Stupid fat moon!

STUPID FAT MOON!

- Stupid Fat Moon

Sitting on the tracks I saw you,
an unsteady ground between us,
both in fear as we burned and ached for
each other.
The crossover—
I sat there on that perch
precarious as it was
and spread the earth
waiting for your Spanish love.
Whether the train came or that forming
sinkhole did swallow me
I'll never know,
as I felt you wrap your arms around me
hotter than the desert sun
that rains down like snow,
and knew that you had conquered your fear
to come find me
and fill my heart with
safety.

- Spanish Love

Rich sienna,
grounded.
A thick paint brush opening the earth,
the artist—weathered garden hands,
dirty fingernails spreading
oil on canvas
the sweetest red, earthy,
a bouquet upon the vine
sharply pleasant, so precise and
unexpected, jolting to the senses
deeply bedded,
sleep.

- Painted Tomatoes

Fireflies
and firelight in your eyes
flickering
a maddening dance.
Lost in the past
with stars in the grass;
gentle passing of time.
Tonight, trace the constellations of the sky
into the creases of my skin
while you hunt for Orion in my eyes
and lay a crown of
Cassiopeia upon my head
and watch as the stars dance
again and again and again.

- Stars in the Grass

Black and white bundles
of Oreo dogs
with hair that does
little tumbleweed tumbles
and tiny cute paws
pitter-pattering, legs scattering,
heart shattering
with the loss of the sound,
wailing like a coon hound.
Beautiful shiny brown eyes
always smiling
and realizing what it truly is to love
a forgiving soul
who makes the world whole
and never asks for more.
Do you forgive me? And my mistakes?
The pain and aches
that went unnoticed,
the stressful appointments,
was it all pointless?
Were you scared?
Did you know that I was there
when I wasn't really there?
Black and white fur,
I really miss her,
her silly ways, her nicknames;
Oreo Cookie and Cookie Crumb
always slipping off my tongue
now left speechless
and broken in pieces.
It all seems so needless.

Crooked teeth and underbites;
the referee to doggy play-fights
and always lighting up my life.
Forever changed and saved my world;
Oreo dog,
best friend, and
baby girl.

- Oreo Dog

Uninspired and tired;
Do these smoky days ever end?
Do these eyes, blinded and stinging,
ever stop drowning in their salty ocean
brine?
Do I have more time?
Or have I reached the end of the line?
Perhaps I'll stay awhile, see where this
road leads another mile,
another step,
and another,
and eventually get to the end.

- The End

Endings are also
beginnings